JOURNEY WITH THE FATHER

A DEVOTIONAL JOURNAL

GLORIA RAYNOR

Published by Victorious You Press™
Charlotte NC, USA

Title: Journey With The Father
First Printed: 2024
Cover Designer: Jadia Bellamy
ISBN: 978-1-959719-29-8

Printed in the United States of America

For details email joan@victoriousyoupress.com
or visit us at www.victoriousyoupress.com

Dedication

Dedicated to individuals who have experienced emotional, physical, spiritual, sexual, and relational hurt. I trust that you will find peace, hope, and joy through the reading of this book coupled with God's word.

CONTENTS

One
YOUR JOURNEY

Before you came from that dark place within your mother's womb, your journey on earth began. There, the Father had his eyes on you and, in determination, has chosen that you do not have to walk alone. And trust me there are days when this walk is very mysterious. Children keep in mind He is waiting for you –your Father. Remember, you have a significant meeting to attend one of these days. There are many memories of meetings, some good, others not, but things have changed. Never give away your heart to another being, except to God, who will never break nor leave you frustrated. Children, love is to mend broken hearts and permeate the spirit of man for fulfillment. God will never give up on those who never give up on him. Use the word of God, the Bible, daily to help you in your spiritual walk.

THE WORD

What is the power of the spoken or written word? It is understanding that the spoken and written word gives strength, life, and hope to anyone who reads it. God is more than able to meet you there.

- The word has the ability to influence the life, and death of things and people.
- Words, when applied effectively, build character and integrity. Still, the effectiveness of the word will manifest once we place action to it. When man understands the wisdom of the spoken and written word through the divine power, minds become renewed, and hearts transformed. Please pay close attention to when we use the word the way the Bible says, there will be no misunderstanding. God told the people to write the word on the tablets of their hearts and teach them and their children not to depart from it. That is why believers must find time to build quality relationships with the word, family, and God, to leave a spiritual legacy for generations.
- Psalm 119:105 KJV. "Your word is a lamp to my feet and a light to my path."
- 2 Timothy 3:16 KJV. "All Scripture, breathed out by God and profitable for teaching, for reproof, for correction, and for training in righteousness.

TODAY'S PRAYER

Heavenly Father, in the name of the Holy Spirit, we yield our bodies, mind, and spirit to you in this hour. Help us to realize that with everything going on, our bodies are the temple of the living God. Holy Spirit, with your assistance, we yield to the Almighty power. God, in the name of Jesus Christ of Nazareth, allow your will in our lives to be done. Father, as we pour out before you, help us to submit our lives into your hands. For darkness seems to be everywhere, and even our government is lost. Please help your people to see how confused and distraught families are in our seasons.

The world is also confused, and the church is bewildered. Lord, there seems to be so much immaturity among us. You have seen the exposure of the unfaithful faith everywhere in the world. The understanding and interpretation of what is happening these days are inconsistent. Today, man has opened the doors to so much evil that it has become uncontrollable. Helps us to realize that only some people who call upon your name will genuinely stand. As we come before you, allow us to recognize that we cannot change them nor your truth. But God assists us to stand for truth in the middle of the chaos. Please give us a heart to love everyone. Lord, I know your word will never change, so help us to lift the standard to suit our King. *Amen.*

Thoughts And Reflections

Or

Write Your Own Prayers

Two

SONGS OF PRAISES

On your daily walk, use these songs of praise to uplift you spiritually and usher the presence of the Lord among you. Trust me, in God's presence, there is fullness of joy with pleasures at His right hand.

A) YOU ARE MY MAJESTY

Lord God, you are my Majesty, and I thank you for redemption.

God of praise, God of hallelujahs, you are awesome in this place.

Lord, I thank you, Father God, as I exalt you, lifting open arms to magnify, worship, and praise your name. Your wonderful work demonstrates your power.

Heavenly Father as I come into your presence let your praise flow through me.

Filling my cup to an overflow for this brand-new day.

To you the center of life I offer up praises in Jesus' name.

All the honor and glory to you my Lord I give. Creator of my life I thank you.

As your creature here on earth I adore, magnify, and worship your holy name. Amen

Lord God Almighty, thank you, for you are perfect in all your ways.

In your presence is where I desire to be.

Lord, even the sinless angels cried Holy, Holy.

Almighty Lord, you are holy; there is no one like you.

Yes, holy, and through the blood of the Lamb in your son Jesus Christ, we too can be holy.

Lord, here I come, for you have afforded me the privilege to call you Abba Father.

Here I am now entering the holies of holies as the righteousness of God through your son Jesus Christ.

Abba Father, I thank and bless your name in Jesus Christ of Nazareth.

Almighty God, thank you for granting me a place in your kingdom.

Have your way, I pray, and your will in our lives this day.

Holy Spirit, lead, guide, and direct my feet to the promised land.

Spirit of the living God, fall afresh on your people this day.

B) COME LET US PRAISE GOD

Come in and praise the Lord.

Come in and praise the Lord.

Let us give Him thanks for his goodness.

Praise Him for his mercy and truth.

Praise Him in the morning as he gives you life.

Come give Him all the glory for saving you.

Come in and praise the Lord.

Give him thanks for waking you up.

Giving you strength for the day, thank Him for the Holy Spirit.

Come and worship him; blessings and honor are entirely due to him, who helps you walk the pathway daily.

Come and worship, blessings, and honor simply due unto him.

Come and worship, blessings, and honor simply due unto him, knowing He is worthy of your praise.

C) BEHOLD THAT NIGHT

Praise God Emmanuel came to Earth.

Praise God Emmanuel came to Earth.

Praise God Emmanuel came to Earth.

Behold! That splendid night with stars beaming across the sky, heaven's radiance outshines Earth.

Bringing down the splendor of heaven.

The Star of David the most spectacular One.

Ushering to Earth the once-in-all eternity most royal occasion birth of the King.

Heaven's royal family gave the most magnificent performance Earth has ever seen.

There, the angels decked out the Milky Ways in royal apparel as that one bright star led shepherds and wise men to his earthly birthplace with a bang.

Behold, it was the most magnificent performance.

Listen, as heaven's choir sang, "Oh, come, let us adore him."

There were angels adorned in royal apparel for that spectacular occasion of the words in the fullness of time. Yes! For the birth of the heavenly King accomplished.

Praise God, born in a lowly manger, came Emmanuel.

Praise God Emmanuel came.

Praise God Emmanuel came.

Praise God Emmanuel came.

D) SATURATE

Lord God Almighty, saturate the atmosphere, we pray.

God, let your glory fill your temple. And fall afresh on us.

Father, please take these earthen vessels and pour your spirit into us.

As we journey through life, help us to seek your truth, knowledge, and wisdom while walking this spiritual path.

Holy Spirit, please apply the purchased, cleansing Blood of the Lamb to our hearts, we pray.

Lord, let your Holy Spirit fill us up as your temple.

Lord, teach us to give honor versus dishonor so that our lives bring glory to you.

Lord, now let your glory fill our hearts.

Lord, let your glory fill our homes.

Lord, let your glory fill our communities.

Lord God, let your glory fill our nations.

TODAY'S PRAYER

What a wonder you are. You light up the skies with your moon and your stars.

Heavenly Father, graciously, you came down to earth to redeem a wretch like me. Father, you are more precious than silver and gold to me. Heavenly Father, your love has given me the courage to go on. You have helped and cared for me like no one else could. My hand is now in your hand. Let your precious fire protect and surround me day and night from life's perils. Savior, precious savior, stay thou nearby me. Precious Father, oh, how I love you.

Heavenly Father, what a wonder you are. You light up the skies with your moon and your stars.

Father, there is no one like you. Thank you for your love. *Amen.*

Thoughts And Reflections

Or

Write Your Own Prayers

Three
UNVEILING OUR TREASURES

Unveiling our treasures before the Lord brings us into His presence. Christ, the way, the truth, and the light, open the door so that we will present our treasures just for Christ. These treasures are precious melodies, honor, worship, and praises we laid up for the Father. Stepping into our treasure rooms helps us not to be afraid. Unveiling our treasures before the Lord creates a connection with our source.

HOW TO BE VESSELS OF HONOR

Being a vessel of honor means being a person of integrity, character, and purpose. It means that you are committed to living a life that is pleasing to God and serving others with humility and respect. Here are some ways to become a vessel of honor:

Seek God's will: Make it a priority to seek God's will for your life. This means constantly communicating with Him through prayer, reading the Bible, fasting, and listening for His voice. When you are in tune with God's will, it equips you to make decisions that honor Him.

Develop a servant's heart: Jesus said, "The greatest among you will be your servant" Matthew 23:11 KJV. Being a vessel of honor means putting the needs of others before your own. Serving them with love and humility as you esteem them above you. Look for opportunities to help others, whether by volunteering, giving to charity, or simply being kind to those around you.

Being a vessel of honor means having good character: It is worth cultivating; this means being honest, trustworthy, and dependable. It also means treating others with respect and kindness, even when they do not deserve it.

Live through purpose, giving your life direction and meaning: Ask God to reveal His purpose for your life and then pursue it with passion and determination. When living purposefully, you will be more fulfilled and better equipped to impact the world around you positively.

To be a vessel of honor, we must be humble: The Bible says to humble yourself under the mighty hands of the Lord God, and he will exalt you. He who exalts himself will always be empty, but he who humbles himself God will exalt in the presence of the enemy.

TODAY'S PRAYER

Shield me, oh Lord, from danger, my God, I pray. Father, shield me from conflicts. Shelter me from the snare of the fowler under your matchless wings. Shield me from the serpent's wrath and his demons in this world. Snatch me from the old dragon's jaws. Shield me, oh Lord. Let me find rest in the safety of your loving arms. Lord, let me find comfort reclining in your bosom.

Let me have your peace even during wars. Let me lean on your breastplate of righteousness and stand on the solid foundation of truth, as a consistent reminder that I can find shelter in you.

Knowing that you, oh Lord, have a home prepared for me. Lord shields me in your presence. Shield me, oh Lord, in your mercy. Shield me in grace through your pardon from my sinful ways. As the danger of this life assails, and the battles intensify, facilitate me to be strong. Help me to depend only on you Father as the fierce winds hold the tides even in the storms of life, beholding the raging waves. Father Divine, I see the spiritual force coming in on every side; shield me this hour, I pray. Yes, in the comfort of your arms, shield me, dear Lord. Shield me, oh Lord, along life's way. Allowing for true comfort that only you can give. Then let me find peace and contentment, knowing you are mine, and I am yours. In the comfort of your arms, shield me, I pray, for in the comfort of your arms, I desire to lie. *Amen.*

Thoughts And Reflections

Or

Write Your Own Prayers

Four

A REMEMBRANCE IN CELEBRATION

Christ is that wonderful gift. It is the date on your calendar every year, December 25. Now accepting his date, you will experience the true joy of the season, for He is the King of Kings. Behold Him in His splendor seated upon his throne. The streets of the home of the King are paved with gold. And the walls around His mansions are of jasper. His Father's mansion has rooms galore. He has offered the extras to those who obey His will and commands: to love the Lord thy God and thy neighbor as yourself. Friends, if we follow His will, we, too, can have a mansion with Christ in paradise.

THE LONELY STAR

Yes, He came as a lonely star but was not alone. The Father, the spirit, and the angelic hosts descended with Him here to earth on that night. Man's plan was for His destruction, but God's plan was to bring us salvation and deliver humanity from sin. Friends, it happened with the best one-time sacrifice of sacrificial blood solution through the blood of the Lamb. Yes, according to the foundational plan He implemented the day Adam and Eve disobeyed His words. God's word in the garden to man was noticeably clear: "*DO NOT.*" A plan utterly different from anything Satan could scheme up to keep redemption quiet, resulting in the bruising and crushing of the serpent's head and heel. In the fullness of time, God sent His only Son to restore man's broken spiritual relationship with the blessed Trinity. And the arrival of the begotten Son fulfilled that promise at the cross.

THE NIGHT OF HIS BIRTH

It was a glorious moment, for heaven was full of splendor. Behold heaven adorned in full majesty as the angels bowed down and worshipped their King. Friend, that night is forever written down in the heaven's registry. Christ the Emmanuel was born on earth, and the best gift to every man, found in a lowly stable. My Friend, it is the costliest gift one can and will ever receive from another man. The gift of eternal life. Oh, so glorious and marvellously packaged and sent down to man. When the newsflash hit the street, all the other kings were curious about who this new King was.

The goonies sent spies to bring back official news about who this King was. Many of them could not even oversee His title, much less His power and divinity: Jesus Christ, the King of the Jews. Immediately, death threats and warrants sent out to bring Him in dead or alive. Wow! Sadly, they had no known clue that they were dealing with the man who gave them life and power. Their lives were in His Father's hand while they sought to take His. Historical documents recorded the many attempts made to put an end to His life. But it was forthcoming, made known in the world that no one can kill the source of all living things. He is the very essence of life. And with that, the conflict between light and darkness continues until such time.

TODAY'S PRAYER

Father, death lingers in our streets. Murder taking place in broad daylight. There is a lack of respect for life, law, property, and even the older people in our neighborhoods. The lawless ones are like puppets in our streets playing the fiddle with innocent lives. God, I know you are out there and have seen it all. Father, here we come, seeking your divine intervention to turn this wrath away. Help us this day, for the earth truly needs you. In Jesus's name, we pray. *Amen.*

Thoughts And Reflections

Or

Write Your Own Prayers

Five
STUCK AT A CROSSROAD

Relationships can be challenging, and sometimes we find ourselves at a crossroad where we need to decide. First, it is important to take some time to reflect on your feelings and the reasons why you are feeling stuck. Are there any specific issues that are causing the roadblock? Communication breakdown, trust issues, or incompatible values can all contribute to feeling stuck.

Once you have identified the root cause of the problem, it is essential to communicate with your partner openly and honestly. Express your concerns, listen to their perspective, and work together to find a solution that works for both of you. If you feel like you need outside help, do not hesitate to reach out to a professional therapist or counselor who can provide guidance and support. Remember, it is okay to take time to evaluate your options and make the best decision for yourself. It is important to prioritize your own happiness and well-being, even if that means making a difficult choice. Ultimately a healthy and fulfilling relationship is built on mutual respect, trust, and communication. Take courage, even the strong feel lost, and unsure at times. Believe in your strength, strive to thrive and not just to survive. Yes, Certified Professional Coaching can help you manage the overwhelms.

IT'S TIME TO HEAL!

Hello there, it is time to heal your Heart and Mind. At LEC Coaching, we offer services that nurture your spirit and help you live, love, and laugh again after pain and abuse. Start living an abundant life by unlocking all that God has in store for you. People, keep in mind the simple words of Christ: "Come as you are." Even though many deep hurts are causing you to put up strong defensive walls and barriers, children, the future is yours. There is absolutely no need to fall prey to the destructive plans of the opponent. Just know that God's grace brings restoration, physically, intellectually, emotionally, and spiritually, by caring and embracing people with love. Remember the simple words of Christ: "Come as you are." even though there are many deep hurts causing you to put up defensive solid wall barriers, children, you are the future.

JESUS YOUR HEALER

The big book tells us that Jesus heals the sick and makes whole those who were blind, weak, and feeble. Children, that is good news about the Kingdom of God for you and me to do charitable deeds. But while Jesus was doing good in the city, the evil men were out to get him because of Satan. Jesus never stops doing good. Then there was that time when a blind man kept calling out his name: "Jesus' son of David show mercy upon me." Jesus' disciples did not like that and kept telling the man to be quiet, but the more they told him, the more he cried. Then Jesus showed compassion and spoke with the man, saying, "What do you want of me?" Opportunity knocked, and the man said that I may receive my sight. Jesus gave him his sight back through his faith and the healing power as seen in "Luke 18:41 KJV.

Children remember that Jesus's power is above the witches and the power of Satan, as written in our books. He is greater than the warlords and all our superheroes. He is the healer and mighty avenger, greater than all the avengers we read about in our storybooks. He is my great hero, and I love Him because He feeds the hungry, heals the sick, gives sight to the blind, and saves my soul from hell.

THE GOOD SHEPHERD

Children, Jesus is also The Great Shepherd, as recorded in Psalm 23. Christ is searching for men, women, boys, and girls to be his Shepherds. Yes, here on earth, to point lost sheep to God at the cross of Calvary. We who were once sinful and have come to know Jesus must tell others of His love so they, too, will find the way as the sheep. As sinners, God wants us to hear His voice, turn from our wicked ways, and serve Jesus. We need to talk to others about Him. Jesus desires us to do good because He came so that man can find the way. John 3:16 KJV says, "For God so love the world that He gave His only begotten son that whosoever believeth in Him should not perish but have everlasting life."

Jesus also tells us about the beauty of life, as seen in how He clothed the lilies, the flowers, and those things on earth that cannot work to feed themselves. Still, as a caring Father, He provides for all. Yes, children, God himself takes care of the little bees, ants, and everything that hath breath, even the trees. We are children created by God, and we must serve him. God created each of us in His image, and we are His creation.

He will provide and care for us as His children when we obey Him. Matthew 6:33 KJV "But seek ye first the kingdom of God, and His righteousness, and all these things shall be added unto you."

Children, everyone who hears and obeys the voice of Jesus will one day live with Him in His mansions. Have you ever wondered how beautiful heaven is? Looking at night at the stars in heaven's galaxies with all the splendor, such beauty blows my mind. I keep telling myself I cannot wait to get to heaven to see Jesus and Daniel. Daniel was a young boy when

God called him, and he promised to be faithful in serving God and God delivered him from the lions.

STOP MASKING YOUR PAIN

Find the root cause of the issue. Implement a strategy to get rid of the issue. Plan, and execute simple and logical solutions in a timely manner to resolve problems. Be consistent and maintain follow up. Please do not allow the darkness to be so consuming that you cannot cry out for help. We offer inspirational communication activities, hope, empowerment, solution, motivational talks on how you go about resolving issues. With positive practical approach: bullying, violence, emotional setbacks, financial imbalance, and hopelessness can resolve.

Visit www.CoachRaynorMinistries.com

TODAY'S PRAYER

Father, I thank you for your goodness. Oh God, help us overcome the double standards in our societies. Our governments have different laws and systems. One is for the rich and elite, another is for the middle class and the poor, and another is for the outcast. But there is no authentic system for those who cannot defend themselves. Father, we, the people, have failed to realize we are the foundation of our societies. And these days, everything is like the flipping of a coin. For we have lost moral values as a people. Heal this land, Lord. *Amen.*

Thoughts And Reflections

Or

Write Your Own Prayers

Six
QUESTIONS TO BE ANSWERED

Which side are you on –the darkness or the light?

How deeply hurt are you?

Why, so much uncertainty taking place in your mind?

From whom are you running?

Why do people come together?

What are you running away from?

How do you choose safety today?

How do you face the true you in the mirror?

Why do so many people find it hard to forgive?

Do you respect yourself as a child of God?

What are you willing to do to overcome the hurt?

How does pain and hurt affects your worship?

How do you respect yourself as a child of God?

How do you show respect to others as a child of God?

How do you develop the discipline to overcome hurts?

How do you show respect to the woman or man coming into your life?

What steps do you take to avoid hindrances in your walk with God?

Now ask yourself the question: do you respect your body as His temple?

How does pain affect you within the body which is the temple of the living God?

Are you willing to develop disciplines to tame your emotions outside of marriage?

Are you willing to allow the Holy Spirit to guide you during your unexpected emotions.?

Whenever your emotions catch you off guard are you still able to stand grounded?

Do You constantly remind yourself that your body is the temple of the living God?

What do you need to yield to God in helping you overcoming insecurity?

How can you challenge your emotions to remain in the spirit and not the flesh?

How can you allow the Holy Spirit to guide you in your emotions to overcome hurt and pain?

What are some of the things causing you to lack a deeper level of intimacy with man and God?

Did you know that taking daily action will benefit you as an individual going through the process of healing?

FORGIVENESS

Forgiving may seem like an awkward thing to do but requires discipline to accomplish it. Then you will rise above the negative impacts and forgive. There are comments which might come up from time to time and refuse to go away. You must create the discipline to free the mind from mental slavery. If you still find it difficult to overcome your hurts and pain, I do hope and trust you continue to rely on the word and Holy Spirit to guide you into all truth. You must develop the discipline and character to act on your hurts to remove hindrance in your emotions.

TODAY'S PRAYER

Father you alone know the intent of man's heart, and so is it written in the word, that the carnal man, cannot understand the ways of God. Now we ask of you heavenly Father to make the heart of man pliable so that he, be receptive to your call when the Holy Spirit speaks. In the name of your Son, help man to realize that there is hope for a better life in knowing you. Father, you have seen our pain and we asked for healing that comes only through you. Bless us we pray as we journey through this day. *Amen.*

Thoughts And Reflections

Or

Write Your Own Prayers

Seven
MY AFFIRMATIONS TO YOU

Give thanks in the morning when you are awake with your emotion intact.

Have a heart of gratitude, always giving thanks for everything.

Lay aside earthly pleasure reminding yourself that your body is first, the temple of the living God.

Allow the Holy Spirit to mentor you in developing intimacy with God, your heavenly Father.

Declare that you will not defile your body with food, fornication, sex, or any emotional activities.

Keep your emotions coordinated daily, by reading the word, meditating, and avoiding the enemy's distractions.

RESTORING RELATIONSHIPS

Keep this in mind: With God, it is never too broken. I do not know where to begin, much, more what to do. Hold on a minute, just come with me; help is on the way.

1. Having the need to understanding your role in the relationship as a man, woman, husband, wife, father, or mother is a very pertinent factor to building relationships.
2. Are you a help meet or a boss?
3. Are you a giver or taker?
4. What have you brought to the table?
5. Are you a parasite or a butterfly?
6. Are you willing to accept responsibilities?
7. Are you a collaborator or an offender defence?
8. How willing are you to apologize or say I am sorry?
9. Make yourself available to listen.
10. Understanding your role in partnership one to the other.
11. Understanding the difference between one who leads and the other who dictates. Keep in mind: to be humble does not diminish the role of a true leader.
12. Understanding partnership roles in relationships is not about masculinity or femininity, it is about the connectivity of two becoming one.

TODAY'S PRAYER

Heavenly Father blessed their union I pray. I give thanks for your kindness towards them. Help them to seek and know that you can provide for their needs. Today I pray for your continuous blessings over their lives. Allow your Holy Spirit to guide and sustain their union.

Holy Spirit I pray your wisdom to guide them to function as one in their relationship. Father now I pray your constant reminder in their ears to continue being faithful to each other. Father let your love flow through their relationship in Jesus' name I pray. *Amen.*

Thoughts And Reflections

Or

Write Your Own Prayers

Eight
SCRIPTURES ON LOVE

Scriptures that help us to better understand our spouses: I chose not to write about them. It is better when you read them for yourself: see the list below, READ, LEARN, and GROW in your relationship with man and Christ.

1 Corinthians 7:33 KJV.

John 13:34-35 KJV loves God and one another.

1 Corinthians 13:4-8 KJV "Charity suffered long and is kind; charity envied not; charity vaunted not itself, is not puffed up,"

1 John 4:18 KJV "There is no fear in love; but perfect love cast out fear: because fear hath torment. And he that walks in fear is not perfect in love."

Solomon 7:13 KJV, and 1 John 4:8 KJV

THE MALE-FEMALE ROLE

The understanding of the male-female role in a marriage is a part of Proverbs 31 KJV: Different responsibility but still on the same page level. Description: Honesty, security, trust, confidence, boldness, integrity, resilient, independent, self-assured, respect, charm, protection, compassion, consideration, great parenting skills, strong character knowledge, caring and understanding unselfish love, spirit of meekness, complementary admiration, attitude of gratitude, thankful submission to each other. This is the kind of love the apostle Paul speaks about in the book of Corinthians to the brethren of Corinth. Authentic love overrides every issue in our lives.

TODAY'S PRAYER

Father helps us as husband and wife to glean on your words that encourage us to esteem others above ourselves. Father, we pray in the name of Jesus Christ your Son to remove selfish pride and ego from us. Help us to see each other as an extension of you. We vow to love and cherish each other as Christ loved the church. Grants us the confidence as husband and wife that we will pray together as we continue to seek your face. Father, we thank you for hearing our prayer. *Amen.*

Thoughts And Reflections

Or

Write Your Own Prayers

Nine
MY SUNRISE MORNING PRAYER

Folks, long before we enter the picture God is doing things on man's behalf. Prayer gets us into the presence of the Father. Jesus Christ the Son of God spent countless hours in prayer. Our role in prayer is participating with God, that His work be done in our lives here on earth as it is in heaven. You must know who you are praying to, and for what you are praying.

In prayer, we must be aware of what God is doing and participate in it. Christ teaches His disciples how to join directly with God through prayer, and not be a spectator but a participator. Prayer can change the course of this world and bring man into the presence of God. Prayer is more than asking God for an outcome; it is about communing with Him in assigned tasks.

Prayer is a means of communicating with God in the awareness that He already knows our needs. Have a look at examples of how Christ goes before the Father in prayer. He goes with an awareness and joins the Father, so that the will of the Father activates in His life. Yes, through the request and petitions made unto God. As believers when we pray from a place of middle person to the Spirit and Son, God will hear and answer us. So, intentionally when we pray, let it be His kingdom come, and His will on earth done. God is already there waiting on us.

Therefore, our sincere attitude towards prayer is knowing God is in control and knows all things. Prayer can direct the course and affairs of this world. Now have a look at John 17 KJV, with regards to the Lord praying for the disciples. Prayer from this angle is our responsibility to adhere to the word as a response to God's ability. Prayer is participating with God through words awaiting his expected outcome.

Our Lord never prays from a passive nor active voice. He always goes to prayer addressing the presence of the Father. One could say He uses the inner voice as if listening and waiting for instruction. Take notice Jesus always prays with awareness of the fact that there is someone in the space before Him, who initiates all things. So, even in prayer Christ actively yields His will to the father. Jesus prays from the position of knowing that God is the one who initiates things and invites us in to participate.

TODAY'S PRAYER

Father transcends your power on us as you might prevail. Father helps us to realize that as we go through life, you are perfect in all your ways. Help your people strive for excellence knowing you do not stand for ordinary. Yes, let your light radiate through us in becoming beams of illumination for this dying world to see you through us. We desire them to know you and become channels for your glory. Almighty One, heaven, and earth is full of your glory, even the galaxies celebrate you. The very moon beam embraces your brilliance. Earth, your creation and your glory, are way beyond the imagination. Still, we are the imperfect perfection in Christ Jesus. Yes, Lord, your glory is beyond man's comprehension. Grant us wisdom as we bask in it all to know your wonders, fill the universe. Lord God saturate our temple with your glory, so we too can exude your ambiance. Father permeates us, yes, in such a way that the world will know you are alive and living inside of us. Allow your light to shine in the darkness, so your children become the light beams transmitting your energy to every man, woman, boy, and girl in Jesus' name. *Amen.*

Thoughts And Reflections

Or

Write Your Own Prayers

GOD'S SIMPLE PLAN OF SALVATION TO US ACCORDING TO THE BOOK OF ROMANS

Man, as a sinner, must admit without God, he is lost. Understand that as a sinner, a crime is committed that deserves the death penalty. Now believe that Jesus Christ died on the cross to save you from sin and death. Saving grace is available for you to repent by turning from your old life of sin to a new life in Christ. Yes, friends, we can receive life through faith in Jesus Christ, God's gift of salvation to the entire universe. Romans 3:9-12, 23, Romans 6:23, Romans 5:8, Romans 10: 9-10, Romans 10:13, Romans 5:1, Romans 8:1. (Taken From KJV)

TODAY'S PRAYER

Abba Father, coming into your presence this hour, please have your way, with my mind, life, and spirit as the giver of my soul. Creator of my life, I surrender to you alone. Holy Spirit, please guide and direct my steps, I pray. Here and now, I yield my life to your divine hand. Master of the Universe, I pray that you help me navigate this maze of life, as I desire to use the navigation manual effectively by accepting that I am the clay in the Potter's hand. Please take me to the Potter's wheel, remold, and melt me as a vessel of honor ready to serve you. As the world's most excellent craftsman, shape and redesign me for your purpose. Allow me to stand firm on the battlefield in Jesus' name. *Amen.*

ABOUT THE AUTHOR

Coach Gloria Raynor is an Ambassador of the King, mother of one daughter and two grandchildren. A Spiritual Counselor, Inspirational Speaker, and writer with three published books" and two more coming out by December. She is a Virtuous Woman who walks in integrity, discipline, and strength. She guides individuals toward restored emotional health, and spiritual awareness, to enhance a balanced lifestyle. As a registered nurse, she strives to let individuals know that God can put together the broken pieces in our lives. Her sensitivity from medical experience allows her to acknowledge the mess in people's lives and hers. She knows that having the right tools; those needs, and mess can clean up. She relies on competent people and God's wisdom to guide her, into a relationship deeply rooted in the understanding covenanted marital vow and commitment with man, the word, and God for satisfaction in life. Folks' true love is beautiful, and the word of God states, the marital bed is undefiled when the parties are faithful to each other emotional and spiritual in a relationship the bond becomes unbreakable. So, it ought to be too, with man's relationship with God the Father.

OTHER BOOKS

Barren with Purpose: Fertility in Dry Places by Gloria Raynor

Christmas Inspiration by Gloria Raynor at https://www.Amazon.com

The Journey with the Father by Gloria Raynor

Mother A Special Pearl: Mothers God's Second Best Gift to humanity, by Gloria Raynor

365 Days Devotional Journal co-author with Vernessa Blackwell

CONTACT

Website: https://www.coachraynorministries.com/

E-mail: loveembraceschange@gmail.com

LinkedIn: https://www.linkedin.com/in/minister-gloria-raynor-6617a3149/

Facebook: https://www.facebook.com/public/Gloria-Raynor

www.ingramcontent.com/pod-product-compliance
Lightning Source LLC
LaVergne TN
LVHW010835120826
845149LV00016B/2742